Break Forth

A Guide to Ignite Your Purpose and Live With Passion

By Lutaline Fosah

Break Forth:
A Guide to Ignite Your Purpose and Live with Passion

By Lutaline Fosah

Manufactured and produced in United States
ISBN Paperback: 9798870228440

Cover design concept: Smiling Eyes Press
Editor: Richard Tardif
Interior Design: Richard Tardif

Imprint: Independently Published

APPRECIATION

To all women who use their light to make sure others have light.

This book is dedicated to my mom and dad, who instilled the values of love and giving back to others and from them, I learnt the values of hard work and dedication in whatever I do in life.

To my husband, Henry Fosah, a dedicated, kind, patient and loving husband who supports me in every way and makes me believe in myself. To my three beautiful and amazing children, Ethan, Kemuel and Elora, who make me want to be a better human and parent. And to every woman who has been my "tribe," holding my hand and believing in me, I thank you.

TABLE OF CONTENTS

INTRODUCTION

INTRODUCTION

HAVE YOU EVER experienced uncertainty, sensing that you have untapped potential to unleash? Do you sometimes find comfort in the shadows, avoiding the spotlight? These feelings may have been fueled by the societal notion that women are primarily suited for domestic roles, leaving you questioning whether there's more to your abilities. Perhaps you've hesitated to embark on your life's purpose, burdened by concerns about how to fulfill it.

But have you considered that you possess unique gifts and talents bestowed upon you by a higher power, ready to be shared with the world? These are questions that deserve your contemplation. Have you dedicated time to unearthing the essence of your existence, or do you frequently ponder, "What is my purpose?" You're not alone. Many women seek guidance in discovering meaning and direction. The uplifting news is that uncovering your genuine purpose and calling is never too late.

The Scriptures offer us the inspiring stories of remarkable women like Deborah, a Prophetess, Judge, mother, and wife (Judges 4:4), who adeptly harmonized spirituality, politics, and family life without compromising her domestic responsibilities. She even led an army into battle. Another awe-inspiring account is that of Esther (The Book of Esther, Chapter Two), who rose to become a queen in a foreign land despite her humble background and various limitations. So profound was her influence that God used her to bring deliverance to Israel.

In Break Forth, you'll embark on a transformative journey to uncover your unique gifts and talents, learning how to leverage them to craft a life teeming with purpose, passion, and fulfillment. Through riveting stories and deep introspection, you'll acquire the tools and confidence necessary to pursue your dreams and positively impact the world.

Whether you aspire to initiate a career change, launch a new business venture, or simply find more joy and fulfillment in your daily life, Break Forth is your guiding light, leading you on this transformative path. Every woman possesses a distinctive gift to offer the world and a calling to fulfill.

However, fear, doubt, and limiting beliefs often shroud us from living our best lives and realizing our full potential. The empowering truth is that you possess the inner strength to break free from these constraints and discover your boundless purpose.

In the pages ahead, we'll delve into the inspiring stories of women who have unearthed their passions and gifts, employing them to construct lives brimming with joy, fulfillment, and meaningful impact. You'll also gain insights into how you can uncover your limitless purpose, irrespective of the obstacles you may encounter on your journey.

Break Forth commences by emphasizing the significance of embracing a sense of purpose and how it can profoundly enhance every facet of your life. You'll explore the science behind why having a life of purpose can lead to increased happiness, improved physical and mental health, and a profound sense of fulfillment. You'll discover how to infuse meaning into your work, relationships, and hobbies.

We'll delve into the barriers that often hinder you from living your best life and realizing your full potential. You'll be equipped with strategies to conquer fear, doubt, and limitations, empowering you to break free from the confines of your comfort zone, shed negative self-talk, and embrace your authentic self, complete with its inherent gifts and talents.

Break Forth will encourage you to celebrate your progress and achievements, embrace change and growth, and sustain your motivation on this transformative journey. In that light, Chapters Nine and Ten will offer questions, tips and exercises to begin your journey toward a life of purpose.

Let's begin.

CHAPTER 1

DISCOVER YOUR LIFE OF PURPOSE

BETTY SAT ALONE under a tree, her eyes red and swollen from crying. She remembered a past conversation with a friend about a choice that backfired. She told her friend, "I turned down a great job that could have elevated my life."

Her friend asked, "What happened?"

"He left me for another," Betty replied.

Why did Betty let herself down in this way?

Why did Betty make the wrong choice?

Was Betty living a life of purpose (LoP)?

It all begs for answers, doesn't it?

Despite its appeal, a LoP may seem challenging, and you might have preconceived ideas. These baked-in ideas often come from family, community, and society. For example, to marry and have children, earn a certain amount of money or achieve a particular position in society.

People often ask me:

"What is a woman's LoP? How do I find it?"

"What are we supposed to do with our lives?"

"What are we here for?"

These are important questions because, as women, we wear many hats—we are mothers, wives, daughters, sisters, friends, and employees. We care for our families, run households, manage careers, and fulfill social obligations. It's easy to get caught up in the day-to-day responsibilities. Although every woman will be different, a woman's LoP is to create, leave her family and friends with more hope, love, and emotional resources, love her passion, and be an example to others. It's finding fulfillment. And it's also to deliver yourself, in your authentic feminine core, to the world—your why.

WHAT DOES A LOP MEAN?

"I know the thoughts that I think towards you; thoughts of peace and not of evil to give you an expected end." (Jeremiah 29: 11).

God has plans for every woman. His plans are good; we must only discover and align ourselves with them. You can't fail when you are in God's will.

Individual goals, passions, and values influence one's sense of direction in life. For some women, this sense may revolve around nurturing happy and healthy children, while for others, it's excelling in their careers or contributing to their communities. This guiding force motivates women to face the world each day. Without it, they might experience feelings of being adrift or unfulfilled, leading to challenges in their mental and emotional well-being.

To a woman, LoP means having a meaningful reason to exist and what she wants to accomplish. It helps a woman define her identity and gives her a sense of fulfillment and satisfaction. It provides a sense of meaning and direction and can be a powerful motivator for a more meaningful and fulfilling life.

It might sound like a nice-to-have, but it's more important than you think. It contributes to better physical health and mental fitness and reduces the risk of chronic disease. Multiple studies have shown that a LoP prolongs one's lifespan.

It comes from feeling connected to others. Using your gifts in the service of others can help, while isolation and loneliness can cause you to have an existential crisis.

Some of us spend our lives searching for meaning, pursuing others' goals, or living within self-imposed limitations. Some find success, while others face setbacks, and there are those who, despite knowing their path, still encounter distractions.

You might awaken with uncertainty, wondering how to fill your days. You've experimented with new hobbies, engaged in volunteer work, deepened your involvement in the church, joined interest groups, or even ventured into entrepreneurship. Yet, that lingering bewilderment remains, leaving you unsure how best to invest your time.

Recognize that a divine hand has crafted you with a specific calling. Your Creator meticulously molded your personality, appearance, mannerisms, strengths, spiritual gifts, natural talents, passions, and every facet of your being to equip you for the unique work He has designated for you to fulfill.

THE SCIENCE OF PURPOSE

Recently, the idea of purpose has emerged as a topic of increasing interest and scrutiny among individuals and researchers. For women, embracing a LoP can yield many benefits, ranging from enhanced brain function and overall physical and mental well-being to increased resilience and a sense of life satisfaction.

But the interaction between purpose and identity is even more profound. Developing one's sense of purpose coincides with developing one's identity and changing identity points (self-doubt, fear of failure and mistakes, lack of support and resources, unreasonable societal expectations, etc.) The field of research focuses on the psychological and physiological effects of having a sense of direction in life. It investigates how a LoP influences our brains, bodies, behaviors, and overall well-being.

In this chapter, we embark on a fascinating journey into the realm of the Science of Purpose. We will explore the connections between purpose-driven living and the latest scientific findings on quality of life and longevity. So, let's embark on this enlightening journey to uncover the profound impact of a LoP on our lives and well-being.

OUR BRAINS, BODIES AND WELL-BEING

Neuroscientists have found that a LoP activates specific brain regions associated with motivation, reward, and goal achievement. The findings suggest a LoP helps the brain release dopamine, a neurotransmitter associated with pleasure and motivation. More dopamine helps us maintain focus, energy, and inspiration to achieve our goals.

Further, studies have shown that a LoP can help protect our brains from cognitive decline and dementia. One study suggested a 30% lower risk of developing Alzheimer's. Having a sense of purpose can also positively affect our physical health. Researchers have found that LoP is associated with lower levels of inflammation, a key contributor to many chronic diseases such as heart disease and cancer. A LoP links to better quality sleep, which is crucial for overall health and well-being.

People are more resilient, less likely to experience depression and anxiety, and more likely to cope with difficult situations and setbacks. We are likelier to seek meaningful connections with others who share our values and goals. It can lead to more fulfilling relationships that give us a sense of belonging and social support.

Allow nothing to hinder your growth—establish standards for yourself and continually redefine them. Your life begins when you decide it does and unfolds with every passing moment; pause, reflect, and take control of it.

You don't need to compare yourself to others or gauge your success by their standards. What truly matters is how you confront challenging moments and persist in adversity.

Take a deep breath, and acknowledge all the small blessings to be thankful for.

Who possesses the power to grant you this authority? Is it me? Your spouse? Parents? Your in-laws?

THE ANSWER IS YOU ALONE.

CHAPTER 2

A Life Filled With Purpose

LIVING A LOP MEANS identifying and pursuing goals and activities that align with one's values, passions, and strengths. It involves breaking free from societal expectations and gender stereotypes and pursuing a path that is authentic and true to one's individuality. It means advocating for gender equality and social justice and using one's skills and influence to make a positive impact in the world. Here's how to live a LoP.

PERSONAL VALUES

Personal values are beliefs and principles that guide our behaviors and decision-making. They reflect what is important to us and what we stand for, and they help us prioritize our actions and choices and influenced by many factors, including our upbringing, culture, and life experiences—honesty, integrity, compassion, and justice, to name a few.

When our values are aligned with our actions, we experience a sense of coherence and meaning in our lives. Conversely, when our values are compromised or contradicted, we may feel a sense of dissonance or inner conflict. We must therefore identify our personal values and strive to align our actions with them.

INTERESTS AND GOALS

Our interests reflect our natural inclinations and curiosities, and they provide opportunities for personal growth and self-expression. They range from hobbies and leisure activities to professional pursuits and career paths: Some common interests include art, music, sports, science, and literature.

Our interests play an important role in shaping our LoP. They provide a sense of direction and motivation, and they help us identify areas where we can make a meaningful contribution. Pursuing our interests, as with our values, can also help us develop skills and expertise that are relevant to our personal and professional goals.

Goals are specific and measurable outcomes that we strive to achieve. They reflect our aspirations and ambitions and provide a roadmap for our actions and choices. Goals can be short-term or long-term and can be related to any area of life, such as career, education, relationships, or health. Some common goals include completing a university degree, starting a business, raising a family, or contributing to a social cause.

SELF-AWARENESS

Self-awareness involves being aware of one's strengths and weaknesses, values and beliefs, and how these factors influence one's choices and actions. For women, self-awareness can play a critical role in personal growth, self-care, and empowerment.

Self-awareness also significantly affects our relationships with others. By understanding their emotions and needs, individuals can communicate more effectively and assertively with their partners, family members, and colleagues.

They can establish stronger boundaries and make informed decisions about with whom they spend time and how they allocate their energy.

UNSTOPPABLE FOCUS

An unstoppable focus helps you prioritize your goals and shape your decisions and emotions that align with your aspirations. Unstoppable women don't perceive setbacks as stopping points. Conversely, women without a clear LoP often find themselves stuck in life, which is unsurprising because they have not connected with their passion. It's akin to a high-powered car with no fuel in its tank.

LIVING A VALUE-BASED LIFE

As you embark on the journey of self-discovery, you'll understand the profound importance of your core values. These intangible aspects of life carry significant meaning and shape our choices, actions, and overall perspective. To illustrate this idea, envision three interconnected circles.

Picture the "outermost circle" as the domain of your should values, including societal or externally imposed expectations and norms. You often encounter values you're expected to embrace because of cultural, familial, or peer influences.

Moving inward, you'll encounter the circle of chosen values. These are the selected few from the "should values" you consciously adopt and prioritize. They represent values that resonate with you and become central to your identity. At the core, you'll find your unique core values, which hold the utmost significance, reflecting your deepest convictions and personal philosophy.

To illustrate this further, let's consider an example: Imagine someone working in a corporate job (outermost circle) where the prevalent "should values" include ambition, competition, and material success. However, upon self-reflection, these individuals find more fulfillment in helping others and contributing to their community.

They then transition to a career in the nonprofit sector (chosen values) because it aligns with their core values of empathy, altruism, and social impact (core values).

INTEGRITY

A LoP embodies ultimate integrity, which is whole and complete. As most women begin to live true to their LoP, many report a surprising increase in synchronicity and serendipity. This process often leads to a more profound sense of trust and faith for most individuals as they discover a greater force at work in the universe beyond themselves, and they play an integral role in that force.

GRACE AND FLOW

According to the dictionary, grace is "the unmerited divine assistance given to man... and people with LoP often report living a grace-filled life." Something unique begins when you commit—the universe orientates to your intentions and commitments.

Rather than fighting against the current, allow grace to lead you to what wants to flow.

Cultivate a positive outlook, actively seek new opportunities, and engage with everything you believe will make a difference. Seek new relationships, nurture existing ones, and build stronger connections. Extend your assistance to the people you love, becoming a role model for your family and friends. Embrace a life filled with curiosity, steering clear of destructive habits while seeking out positive ones to make a meaningful impact on the world.

CHAPTER 3

BEGINNING TO BREAK FORTH

THERE IS ALWAYS something that adds passion to your life, maybe when you see someone dancing or singing. You rejoice in it and want to jump in. How can a woman find that? If I may, I am empowering women and girls to become who God has called and granted them to become. Seeing them let go of their self-doubts, fears, limiting beliefs and boundaries, I feel so much joy. What adds passion to your life? In this section, I will share some of the most common ways to help you Break Forth.

WHAT ARE YOU PASSIONATE ABOUT?
As the saying goes, do what you love and love what you do. For example, do you love cooking, cycling, boxing, designing, styling, make-up, teaching, writing, singing, and so on? Entrepreneurs, for example, are a bunch of passionate people who chose to swim against the tide and made their mark just because they love what they do. Pick what you love to do, and think about it.

Maybe you're not doing that right now, and maybe you wanted to be a pianist and ended up being an architect. You're earning well and taking care of every need but don't feel content about it. Ask yourself, what do you miss? Do you miss singing classes, for example, which you had to drop right after you went to high school due to the increased load of studies. Sound familiar? It can be challenging to know what we are truly passionate about and where our natural talents lie.

Here are seven tips to help you discover your passions and talents.

1. **Self-reflection:** Self-reflection is an essential step in discovering your passions and talents. Start by asking some critical questions about what brings you joy, what you enjoy doing in your free time, and what makes you feel fulfilled. Consider your natural strengths and abilities and tasks that come easily to you. Pay attention to activities that absorb you entirely and make you lose track of time, causing you to forget about the world around you. It could be anything from reading, writing, or cooking to gardening, sports, or traveling. Jot down your answers and use them as a starting point for exploring your passions and talents further.

2. **Explore new experiences**: One of the most effective methods to discover your passions and talents is by exploring new experiences. Attend various events, enroll in classes, or try new hobbies you have never engaged in before. You only know what you'll enjoy once you give it a try. When you try something new, you may discover hidden talents or find a new passion—step outside of your comfort zone and explore new experiences regularly.

3. **Pay attention to your emotions:** Pay attention to your emotions in your day-to-day life. Notice when you feel excited or passionate about something and when you feel bored or uninterested. Listen to your intuition and gut instincts; they can help you identify what truly matters to you. If you find yourself dreading a particular task or activity, it may be an indicator that it's not aligned with your passions and talents.

4. **Seek feedback:** Seek feedback from others, especially those who know you well: Friends, family, or coworkers. Ask them about

your strengths and weaknesses and what they believe you are good at. Sometimes, others can see our talents and passions more than we can ourselves. Use their feedback to identify potential areas of interest.

5. **Take assessments:** Consider utilizing assessments or personality tests to help you identify your strengths, weaknesses, and areas of interest. Some popular assessments include the Myers-Briggs Type Indicator (MBTI), the CliftonStrengths assessment, or the Enneagram. These assessments can provide valuable insights into your personality, work style, and interests.

6. **Experiment:** Experiment with various activities and hobbies to discover what resonates with you. Consider volunteering for a cause you're passionate about or enrolling in a class that aligns with your interests. Continuously try new things until you find something that excites you and brings a sense of fulfillment.

7. **List of your accomplishments and achievements:** Make a list of your accomplishments and achievements, both big and small. Celebrate your successes and reflect on what made them possible. Identify what you enjoyed about the experience and what skills you used to achieve your goal.

CONNECT WITH LIKE-MINDED PEOPLE

It is often said, "You are who you surround yourself with."

If you have heard me speak or attended my events, you may recall that I often ask, "Who is in your tribe? Who are the women or friends you keep around you? Are they those who will speak life, encourage and cheer for you and also correct you with love, or are they people who are only here to gossip, cry or complain without solutions or ideas? Do you have someone you can call at midnight to pray on your behalf? If you don't, it's time you found someone, and if you have the wrong friends who are always negative, then it's time to start pruning. Connecting with like-minded people helps you look in a different direction, helps you to learn new things, and also tries to push you to follow your passion; you feel encouraged and determined. You can choose to join discussion forums online, and there are various platforms available.

SPEND TIME ALONE

While you're still connecting to like-minded people, spending time alone gives you time to pause and reflect. It's easy to push your thoughts aside when you're caught up in daily household chores and caring for your children. You might go through a lot of confusion and dilemma. If you feel stuck, refer back to the earlier exercise and ask questions until you're confident of what you want. Take your time and avoid stressing out.

Time alone allows us to evaluate ourselves, where we stand and how skilled we are at criticizing others. It is always easy to judge others but very difficult to evaluate and upgrade themselves. It is never too late. If you have a clear objective in your life, then nothing can stop you.

You need to live the life you imagined for yourself. You will clear all the blockage in your mind, and that is only possible through unlocking your full potential. For example, reading inspiring books. Books have the power to inspire and change your perspective. They will not only help you develop your thought process but will take you to another world of unlimited possibilities.

Or how about maintaining a daily journal? A daily journal is like your mood tracker, growth tracker, and your progress tracker. Writing your thoughts and feelings can be beneficial because you'll evaluate your thoughts and keep a tab on your daily emotions and tasks.

*

While discovering one's LoP can be a fulfilling and empowering experience, it's not always an easy journey. There are obstacles that women may face. In this section, we'll explore some of these obstacles and offer strategies for overcoming them.

SELF-DOUBT

Self-doubt is a common obstacle that women face when trying to discover their purpose. They may question their abilities, talents, or worthiness to pursue their passions or dreams. Self-doubt can stem from a lack of confidence, past failures, or negative feedback from others.

To overcome self-doubt, women can start by acknowledging and challenging their negative thoughts and beliefs. Women can practice positive self-talk and focus on their strengths and accomplishments. Seeking feedback and support from trusted friends, family members, or mentors can also help build confidence and overcome self-doubt.

IMPOSTER SYNDROME

It's not an actual mental health condition. But this term (imposter phenomenon, fraud syndrome, or imposter experience) describes someone who feels they aren't as capable as others think and fears they'll be exposed to be a fraud.

Imposter syndrome can present significant obstacles for women who strive to break free from limitations. Women may experience doubts about their abilities, feel like they don't belong in their roles or fields, and struggle with confidence and self-esteem.

LACK OF SUPPORT

Women may also face obstacles when they lack support from those around them. This can include family members, friends, or colleagues who don't understand or value their goals and aspirations. Lack of support can lead to feelings of isolation, discouragement, or even abandonment.

To overcome a lack of support, women can seek out like-minded individuals who share their passions and goals. They can do this by joining clubs or groups, attending conferences or workshops, or seeking out mentors who can provide guidance and support. Networking and building relationships with others in their field can also help create a supportive community.

SOCIETAL EXPECTATIONS

Women may feel pressure to conform to traditional gender roles or societal norms that limit their potential or discourage them from pursuing their passions, facing discrimination, bias, or stereotypes that undermine their abilities or worth.

Women can challenge gender norms and stereotypes by speaking up and advocating for their rights and opportunities. They can seek out role models and mentors who have overcome similar obstacles and succeeded in their chosen fields. They can also support and uplift other women and help create a more inclusive and equitable society.

RESOURCES

Women may face obstacles when they lack the necessary resources in the pursuit of a LoP, for example, financial resources, educational opportunities, or access to technology or networks. A lack of resources can limit their ability to explore new options, gain new skills, or connect with others.

To overcome the lack of resources, women can seek out scholarships, grants, or other financial aid programs that can help fund their education or training. They can also benefit from free or low-cost resources, such as online courses, libraries, or community centers. Networking and building relationships with others in their field can also help open doors to new opportunities and resources.

CHAPTER 4

BREAK FORTH FROM YOUR COMFORT ZONE

THE ACCEPTED DEFINITION OF a comfort zone is "a psychological state in which things feel familiar to a person, and they are at ease and in control of their environment, experiencing low levels of anxiety and stress." Therefore, we can assume that stepping out of one's comfort zone will raise anxiety and generate stress, so much pressure that returning to that zone of familiarity is easier and safer.

Stepping beyond it allows us to learn, grow, and explore new opportunities on our journey to a LoP. The reward is a sense of empowerment from knowing you have the courage and strength to pursue your goals.

This chapter will guide you to Breaking Forth from your comfort zone, addressing its associated fears, self-doubt, the limiting beliefs and boundaries that hold us back, and overcoming these limits.

HOW TO BREAK FORTH
Moving from the "heart" of your comfort zone to the vast empire of possibilities that await outside requires us to embark on a journey of breaking forth. This journey is crucial for women, empowering them to step beyond their comfort zones and explore new horizons.

Let's look into practical steps to assist us in breaking free from the confines of our comfort zones. These approaches will help us embrace change, challenge ourselves, and tap into the confidence and resilience needed to thrive in unfamiliar territories.

> **Start small**: Try something new, like picking up a new hobby or taking a class in a subject that interests you. As you grow comfortable with these small challenges, you will move on to more significant challenges.

> **Set goals and embrace failure:** Failure is an inherent part of the journey when breaking forth. Embrace failure. It is essential to remember that failure does not define your worth or abilities.

> **Surround yourself with supportive people:** Seek out people who will provide encouragement and support as you pursue your goals and dreams. Conversely, avoiding those who are negative or discouraging is advisable because they may impede your progress.

> **Try new experiences and take calculated risks**: Step outside of your daily routine and try something new, like trying a new restaurant or traveling to another country. As you try new experiences, you will discover new passions and interests. Identify risks that are worth taking and weigh the potential outcomes. Take steps to mitigate the risks, such as doing your research or seeking advice from others. Remember that calculated risks can lead to significant rewards.

OVERCOMING THE FEAR OF BREAKING FORTH

The fear of Breaking Forth is a shared experience—an overwhelming feeling that hinders women from reaching their potential and pursuing their dreams. This fear can stem from various factors, including societal expectations, self-doubt, and experiences.

> **Recognize and acknowledge fear:** The first step is to acknowledge it. Many women often deny or suppress their fear, which only makes it worse. It is important to acknowledge that it is a natural emotion and often linked to failure. Recognize that fear is not unique to women and that everyone experiences them.

> **Understand the root cause of your fear:** Fear can be caused by a variety of factors, including past experiences, societal expectations, and self-doubt. Take the time to reflect on why you are feeling scared and try to identify the underlying cause.

> **Change your mindset:** It is important to adopt a growth mindset and believe that you can achieve anything you set your mind to. Shifting perspective from seeing failure as a negative outcome to recognizing the opportunity to learn and grow will be necessary. When you adopt a growth mindset, you will be more willing to take risks and pursue your dreams.

> **Create a plan:** This plan should include clear goals, timelines, and actionable steps that will help you achieve your goals. Break your plan down into small, manageable steps, and celebrate your accomplishments along the way—this will help you build momentum and stay motivated.

> **Confront your fear:** Identify the barriers holding you back and then plan to overcome them. Start small by setting achievable goals and working towards them. You will gain confidence in your abilities and start to see yourself in a more positive light.

> **Practice self-care:** Take the time to care for your physical, emotional, and mental health. This will involve getting enough sleep, eating healthy foods, exercising, and engaging in activities that bring you joy. When you take care of yourself, you will be better equipped to overcome your fears.

OVERCOME SELF-DOUBT TO BREAK FORTH

Breaking Forth can be daunting as societal pressures can lead to self-doubt and feelings of inadequacy. However, with the right mindset and tools, it is possible to overcome these doubts and achieve success.

> **Recognize and address your self-doubt:** One effective way to address self-doubt is to challenge negative thinking with evidence to the contrary. For example, if you believe, "I am not good enough to achieve my goals," challenge it by listing your achievements and accomplishments.

> **Focus on your strengths:** Focusing on your strengths will help combat those feelings of self-doubt. Make a list of your strengths and talents, and refer back to this list whenever you start to doubt yourself. Understand that everyone has weaknesses. Instead of fixating on your weaknesses, focus on your strengths and find ways to utilize them to pursue your goals. By leveraging your strengths, you can maximize your potential and make significant progress toward achieving what you set out to accomplish.

> **Stay motivated:** Staying motivated can be challenging, especially when faced with obstacles. One effective strategy is to set realistic and achievable goals. Break down larger goals into smaller, more manageable tasks, and track your progress.

LIMITING BELIEFS

These are beliefs that limit our potential and prevent us from leaving our comfort zones. They can be about ourselves, our abilities, or the world around us. For example, you may believe that you are not smart enough to pursue a certain career or that you are not attractive enough to find a partner—these beliefs can prevent us from taking risks, trying new things, and pursuing our passions.

Limiting beliefs can develop from past experiences, societal expectations, and negative self-talk. Societal expectations, for example, can be significant factors. We have been told, in many cases, that we are not as capable as men and that we should prioritize our families over our careers. These messages can lead to self-doubt and negative beliefs about ourselves and our abilities. Recognize the beliefs that are holding you back.

> **Acknowledge them**: Ask yourself if these beliefs are true and if there is evidence to support them. One challenge is to replace negative thoughts with positive ones. Instead of telling yourself that you are not good enough, focus on your strengths and accomplishments. Remind yourself of times when you had challenges and succeeded.

> **Take small steps:** Take small steps to build confidence gradually. Begin with something slightly outside and work your way up. For instance, if you are afraid of public speaking, start by speaking in front of a small group of friends or colleagues.

> **Practice self-compassion:** Practice self-compassion and be kind to yourself when working to overcome your limiting beliefs— remember that changing deeply ingrained beliefs takes time and effort. Celebrate your successes and be patient with yourself as you work towards your goals.

OVERCOME LIMITING BOUNDARIES

Often, our limited boundaries pins us to the mat of our comfort zones—these types of beliefs refer to the constraints that prevent individuals from achieving their full potential. These constraints can come in different forms: Lack of opportunities, resources, and societal expectations. In this section, I will show you how to overcome limited boundaries.

> **Embrace diversity:** Embracing diversity will help you overcome limited boundaries. Celebrate differences and seek out opportunities to learn from people with diverse backgrounds and

experiences—create inclusive environments where everyone feels valued and respected.

> **Seek out opportunities:** One of the primary effects of limiting boundaries on personal growth is the lack of opportunities available to women. Women may face barriers and be deprived of education, employment, or leadership opportunities. As a result, they might be unable to develop their skills and talents.

LIMITING BOUNDARIES ON PERSONAL GROWTH

Limiting boundaries can have a significant impact on the personal growth of women. These boundaries can be societal, cultural, or individual, and they can prevent women from reaching their full potential.

Women who face limiting boundaries may also suffer from a lack of self-confidence. They may have internalized beliefs that they are not good enough or that they cannot achieve their goals. This can lead to a lack of self-confidence, which will further reinforce limiting boundaries.

Women must recognize their strengths and talents and work to develop and utilize them to achieve their goals. This can be achieved through self-reflection, positive self-talk, and continued support from others.

The effects limiting boundaries can also have negative health effects on women. We are facing limitations and barriers that can lead to feelings of frustration, hopelessness, and inadequacy. It can also increase stress levels, leading to anxiety and depression.

*

Now that you are Breaking Forth from your comfort zones, you're recognizing that you are capable of achieving more than possible. This new found self-confidence can carry over into other areas of your life and help you to take on more significant challenges.

It's beneficial to start with manageable objectives and work steadily towards accomplishing them. Your self-assurance will naturally increase, and you will perceive yourself more positively. Although it may seem daunting, taking those first steps outside your comfort zone is vital. Embracing new challenges and seizing new opportunities will propel you to self-discovery and achievement.

CHAPTER 5

INSPIRING STORIES

IN THIS CHAPTER, I will explore the inspiring stories of women who have overcome obstacles and achieved greatness in various fields, including science, politics, literature, sports, and activism. Through their stories, we will gain insight into the struggles and triumphs of women throughout history and appreciate the incredible resilience and determination that these women possess.

WOMEN IN POLITICS

One of the most inspiring women in politics is Vice-President Kamala Harris. She made history in 2021—the first female, first African-American, and first Asian-American Vice President of the United States. Harris started her career as a prosecutor and served with the California Attorney General before being elected to the U.S. Senate in 2016. She is known for her firm stance on social justice issues and active advocacy for women's rights, LGBTQ+ rights, and racial justice.

Another inspirational woman in politics is Jacinda Ardern, the Prime Minister of New Zealand since 2017. Ardern is recognized for her empathetic leadership style and focus on social issues like poverty, housing, and mental health. She received praise for responding to the 2019 Christchurch mosque shootings, which claimed 51 lives. Ardern promptly condemned the attack and expressed solidarity with the Muslim community. She also implemented gun control laws in response to the attack, a move widely commended.

WOMEN IN SCIENCE

Traditionally male-dominated, science has seen significant contributions from women in recent years. One inspiring woman in science is Jennifer Doudna, who received the Nobel Prize in Chemistry in 2020 for her groundbreaking work on CRISPR-Cas9 gene editing. Doudna and her colleagues developed a precise gene-editing technique that will be revolutionary in medicine and agriculture.

Another influential figure in the realm of science is Katie Bouman. She led the team that successfully captured the first image of a black hole in 2019. Bouman devised an algorithm that enabled the team to gather data from multiple telescopes to create the historical image. She has become a role model for young girls interested in science, inspiring more women to pursue STEM careers.

WOMEN IN BUSINESS

The business world has historically been male-dominated, but women have made significant strides in recent years. One inspiring business person is Ursula Burns, who achieved the historic milestone of becoming the first Black woman to lead a Fortune 500 company. Burns was the CEO of Xerox from 2009 to 2016 and is renowned for her emphasis on innovation and diversity. She has been a vocal advocate for increasing the representation of women and minorities in leadership roles, mentoring many young professionals throughout her career.

Another influential figure in the business world is Sheryl Sandberg, former Chief Operating Officer at Facebook. Sandberg is recognized for her dedication to promoting gender equality in the workplace and has authored several books on the topic, including Lean In: Women, Work, and the Will to Lead. Additionally, Sandberg established the

Lean In Foundation, which offers resources and support to women in their professional endeavors.

WOMEN IN SPORTS

Sports have traditionally been male-dominated, but women have made significant strides in recent years. One inspiring woman in sports is Simone Biles, considered one of the greatest gymnasts ever. Biles has won 30 Olympic and World Championship medals, including 23 gold medals. She is known for her incredible athleticism and ability to perform complex gymnastic moves efficiently.

Another remarkable woman is Billie Jean King, a tennis player born in 1943 in California. King began playing tennis at a young age and quickly rose to become one of the best players in the world. In 1973, King participated in the famous Battle of the Sexes match against Bobby Riggs, a male tennis player who had claimed that women were inferior in sports. King defeated Riggs in straight sets, and the match became a landmark for gender equality in sports.

King's victory helped shatter gender stereotypes and paved the way for future generations of women athletes. Her legacy continues to this day.

WOMEN IN LITERATURE

One such woman is Mary Shelley, the author of the famous novel "Frankenstein." Shelley was born in 1797, and despite losing her mother at an early age, she received a formal education from her father, a philosopher and writer. At 18, Shelley eloped with the poet Percy Bysshe Shelley and traveled throughout Europe. During this time, she wrote "Frankenstein," considered one of the greatest works of English literature.

Frankenstein tells the story of a scientist who creates a monster and explores themes of ambition, responsibility, and the consequences of playing God. Shelley's novel challenged societal norms of the time, which viewed women as passive and submissive. Frankenstein has been adapted into various forms, including movies, TV shows, and plays. Her work has inspired generations of writers and readers, leaving an immeasurable impact on literature.

Another woman who broke through in literature is Toni Morrison. Morrison was born in 1931 in Ohio and grew up in a racially segregated society. Morrison excelled academically and earned a degree in English from Howard University. After working as an editor for several years, Morrison began writing her novels, which explored the experiences of African Americans. Her most famous book, Beloved, tells the story of a formerly enslaved person haunted by the memory of her dead child.

Morrison's work challenged the literary canon, long dominated by white male authors. Her novels explored themes of race, gender, and identity, giving voice to marginalized communities. Morrison's impact on literature has been immense, and she has received numerous awards and honors, including the Nobel Prize in Literature. Her work continues to be read and studied.

*

These heralds of the business world share two essential traits: Determination and resilience. Determination embodies drive, persistence, and unwavering commitment when striving to achieve a goal or surmount an obstacle. It entails the capacity to set objectives, devise a plan, and persevere, regardless of setbacks or challenges that may arise.

Resilience involves the capacity to rebound from adversity, stress, or trauma. For instance, someone determined to complete a marathon might encounter setbacks like injuries or unexpected life events that disrupt their training schedule. However, if they have resilience, they can bounce back, adapt their training regimen and continue working toward their goal.

These outcomes represent the transformative results of a determined individual's journey. Let's focus on five essential transformations of determination: Increased diversity and representation, economic empowerment, improved self-confidence, and enhanced decision-making skills.

1. **Determination:** Generally, determination is a positive emotion that promotes perseverance toward a goal despite obstacles. Determination occurs before goal attainment and motivates behavior to help achieve one's LoP, leading to the following benefits.

2. **Increased diversity and representation:** When women are determined, they help increase diversity and representation in various fields and industries, particularly in areas where women have been historically underrepresented, such as STEM fields, politics, and business. It contributes to a broader range of perspectives and ideas, benefiting society.

3. **Economic empowerment**: Women determined to Break Forth and pursue their goals can achieve economic empowerment and attain financial stability and independence while pursuing higher-paying and more fulfilling careers. By breaking through barriers and achieving success, women can access opportunities and resources previously unavailable, reducing gender-based income disparities and fostering economic growth and development.

4. **Improved self-confidence:** Imagine someone determined to become a published author. When they write and submit their work to publishers, they will receive feedback that may be positive or negative. However, even in the face of rejection, they will maintain belief in their abilities and vision. Over time, this confidence will grow, making them more self-assured in their ability to achieve their goals.

5. **Improved decision-making skills:** Determination requires individuals to make difficult decisions and take calculated risks, helping them develop their skills and grow comfortable with risk-taking. This, in turn, enables individuals to make better decisions in all aspects of their lives. For example, someone deter-

mined to start their own business must make various decisions, such as product offerings, pricing, and marketing strategies.

RESILIENCE

The American Psychological Association defines resilience as "the process of adapting well in the face of adversity, trauma, tragedy, threats, or significant sources of stress." When individuals are determined, they develop a strong sense of resilience because they focus on their goals and are willing to overcome any obstacles that may stand in their way. Now, let's delve into the significance of resilience, examining its effects on mental well-being, career achievements, personal fulfillment, and identifying role models.

> **Impact of resilience on mental health**: Women determined to Break Forth and achieve their goals may encounter setbacks or failures that can be challenging to cope with. However, if they are resilient, they will be better equipped to manage the stress and anxiety that comes with these challenges, developing healthier coping mechanisms. Resilience can also help women develop a positive mindset and outlook, which benefits overall mental health and well-being.

> **Career success:** Resilience is pivotal in achieving career success, particularly for women navigating the complex workplace. Women often encounter numerous challenges and limited opportunities for advancement, making the capacity to surmount these hurdles crucial for success. Furthermore, limited options can stifle professional growth, leading to frustration and stagnation. However, resilience empowers women to confront these challenges, persevere, and strive for excellence despite obstacles. Resilience in the context of career success involves bouncing back from setbacks and proactively seeking solutions to break through barriers. It enables women to advocate for themselves and negotiate fair compensation.

> **Personal fulfillment:** Resilience holds immense significance for personal fulfillment among women, enabling them to pursue their passions and dreams, whether related to health, relationships, or personal development. Overcoming setbacks and obstacles becomes pivotal in achieving these aspirations, even when facing challenges related to time management, self-doubt, or a lack of support. Resilience is the key to surmounting these challenges and maintaining an unwavering focus on their goals, even in adversity.

> **Identifying role models:** Role models are individuals who have succeeded in areas that hold significance for you and can offer guidance and motivation to pursue your objectives. When seeking out role models, it is crucial to search for individuals who share your values and goals and who have surmounted challenges and obstacles similar to those you may encounter. For instance, if you aspire to Break Forth in science, you may seek accomplished role models. Once you pinpoint role models who inspire you, delve into their experiences and glean insights from their strategies—reading biographies or interviews, attending talks or presentations, or connecting with them through social media or professional networks.

CHAPTER 6

NINE INSPIRATIONAL SUCCESS STORIES

IF YOU'RE SEEKING INSPIRATION, this is the place to be. These nine incredible success stories by famous writers, entrepreneurs, and creators will serve as a great source of motivation.

OPRAH WINFREY

Oprah Winfrey is America's most influential woman. She overcame many obstacles, including being raised in poverty and enduring years of abuse. However, after moving in with her father, Winfrey conquered the trauma and became an honors student with a full college scholarship.

While still in her sophomore year, she began her career as a news anchor at CBS Nashville. This marked just the beginning of her successful journey. She ascended to the TV industry, eventually becoming America's favorite television personality. Today, Winfrey serves as the CEO and founder of Harpo Productions.

JK ROWLING

JK Rowling's journey began as a single mother on welfare. JK Rowling was the first person to think of the idea of a young wizard traveling on a delayed train from London to King's Cross Station.

She began to write on scrap paper and slowly developed the story. For five years, publishers rejected her manuscript of Harry Potter & the Philosopher's Stone before it was accepted by Bloomsbury Publishing.

Harry Potter was a success story that shaped a whole generation of children. It sold over 500 million copies in total worldwide and made Rowling the world's first billionaire author. Yet, in a testament to her values, she donated a substantial portion of her fortune to charitable causes and relinquished the billionaire title, embracing a new chapter dedicated to philanthropic endeavors.

ANITA RODDICK

The success of The Body Shop's late founder, Anita Roddick, could not have been predicted. Roddick had a simple goal when she founded The Body Shop—to sell cruelty-free cosmetics made with natural ingredients. After opening her first store in 1976 in New York, it was a huge success that led to many franchises. By 1991, there were over 700 stores worldwide.

Roddick's vision made The Body Shop a leader in ethical consumption. It was one of the first companies to ban animal-tested ingredients and promote fair trade products. Roddick used her thriving business to advocate for many environmental and social causes. She often worked with organizations like Greenpeace.

SARA BLAKELY

Sara Blakely aspired to become a lawyer. She failed the LSAT exam twice, receiving a lower score the second time. Feeling defeated, she took a job at Disney World before eventually moving back home with her mother.

After working in fax machine sales for seven more years, Blakely had her Eureka! After altering her pants' feet to fit in white jeans, she saw a new product opportunity. Despite struggling to find a manufacturer willing to collaborate on the project for months, Blakely persevered and became a successful entrepreneur.

She built a multibillion-dollar shapewear company based on a simple yet ingenious idea.

DOLLY PARTON

Dolly Parton, the fourth of twelve children, grew up in rural Tennessee, where she shared a bed with her siblings and three to four other children. These were humble beginnings, but Parton attributes her success, despite her family's financial difficulties, to the love and support of her parents. Her mother, Avie Lee Owens, was a singer and guitarist who frequently entertained her children with her talents, while her father, Robert Lee Parton, played banjo and guitar.

At the age of five, she wrote her first song, and two years later, she built her first guitar using a mandolin and two guitar strings. Her uncle, Bill Owens, played a pivotal role in helping her launch her career, and she had her first gig at the Home Hour and The Cas Walker Farm in Knoxville when she was only ten.

Parton is now a legend in country music, a showbiz icon, and a multimillionaire who uses her resources to help others. Throughout her career, she has been a passionate supporter of philanthropy, contributing to environmental conservation and childhood literacy.

In 1995, she created the Imagination Library, a program that sends free books to children worldwide. In 1988, Parton established the non-profit Dollywood Foundation to provide scholarships for high school students.

HALLE BERRY

Halle Berry was born and raised in Ohio. Her father's abusive behavior towards her mother led to her mother's decision to divorce, raising her and her siblings alone. Despite her challenging upbringing, Berry excelled at cheerleading and was an honor student. She also participated in several beauty pageants, placing sixth in 1986.

In pursuit of an acting career, Berry moved to New York City. However, she faced financial hardships, and her aspirations left her struggling as an artist, even leading her to spend a few days living in shelters. Eventually, she relocated to Los Angeles, where her acting journey took off.

MAYA ANGELOU

Maya Angelou was an American poet, memoirist, and civil rights activist, best known for her autobiography, "I Know Why the Caged Bird Sings." Angelou's life was marked by poverty, racism, and abuse, but she discovered solace and purpose in writing and creativity.

Through her writing, Angelou explored themes of identity, race, and gender, becoming a prominent voice in the civil rights movement. She also worked as a dancer, singer, and actress and passionately advocated education and literacy.

Angelou's journey teaches us that finding purpose involves pursuing our passions and utilizing our talents to make a difference in the world. Whether through writing, art, or activism, we can find fulfillment and meaning by following what we love and sharing our gifts with others.

MALALA YOUSAFZAI

Malala Yousafzai is a Pakistani activist for female education and the youngest Nobel Prize laureate. Her journey began when she started advocating for girls' education at 11 and continued after surviving an assassination attempt by the Taliban in 2012.

Despite her dangers, Yousafzai persisted in speaking out for education and equality, becoming a global icon for human rights. She subsequently founded the Malala Fund, which supports education initiatives for girls worldwide.

Yousafzai's journey teaches us that finding purpose involves standing up for our beliefs and fighting for what is right. By using our voices and advocating for change, we can make a meaningful difference in the world and find fulfillment in our lives.

ELLEN DEGENERES

Ellen DeGeneres, an American comedian, talk show host, and actress, has emerged as an icon of kindness and compassion. In 1997, she embarked on a significant journey, garnering support when she publicly came out as a lesbian. This revelation sparked controversy and significant media backlash. Despite her challenges, DeGeneres wholeheartedly embraced her authenticity and used her platform to advocate for kindness and compassion.

She has become a strong advocate for various causes, including animal rights, LGBTQ+ rights, and mental health awareness. DeGeneres has leveraged her wealth and influence to support charitable initiatives worldwide. DeGeneres's journey teaches us that discovering one's purpose involves embracing our authentic selves and promoting compassion and kindness in the world.

These stories remind us that finding purpose involves perseverance, passion, and the courage to overcome adversity.

CHAPTER 7

DEVELOPING A GROWTH MINDSET

A GROWTH MINDSET IS a belief system that posits that one's abilities, intelligence, and talents can be developed through persistent effort, dedication, and perseverance. These individuals believe success depends on hard work, continuous learning, and a readiness to confront challenges.

The accomplishments of others are a source of inspiration. They are inclined to draw lessons from their peers. Failure is an opportunity for growth and to exhibit greater resilience. Conversely, a fixed mindset represents a belief system based on the notion that one's abilities, intelligence, and talents are unchangeable traits. Those with a fixed mindset focus on achieving specific outcomes, such as high grades or promotions, and may hesitate to invest in the learning process if they doubt the desired outcome. They avoid challenges, eschew constructive feedback, and readily surrender when facing obstacles.

Let's have a closer look at their differences.

BELIEFS ABOUT ABILITIES
Individuals with a growth mindset believe in the potential for abilities to evolve, while those embracing a fixed mindset adhere to the belief that ability remains static. Those with a growth mindset perceive

challenges as opportunities for learning and personal development, whereas individuals with a fixed mindset view challenges as threats to their innate abilities.

APPROACH TO LEARNING

People with a growth mindset tend to concentrate more on the learning process, while those with a fixed mindset focus primarily on the result. Those with a growth mindset derive enjoyment from the act of learning itself and are more inclined to engage in deliberate practice to enhance their skills. Those with a fixed mindset are more preoccupied with achieving specific outcomes, such as high grades or promotions. They may be less willing to invest in the learning process if they believe the desired outcome is uncertain.

REACTION TO FAILURE

Individuals with a growth mindset typically view failure as an opportunity for learning and are more likely to persevere in the face of setbacks. In contrast, those with a fixed mindset often interpret failure as a reflection of their inherent abilities and may be more prone to giving up when confronted with obstacles.

Failure is an inevitable part of learning and growth, and it provides valuable feedback and information about your performance. Instead of fearing or becoming discouraged by failure, adopt a positive attitude toward it and see it as a natural part of the learning process."

Rather than viewing failure as a reflection of your abilities or worth as a person, view it as an opportunity to learn and grow. Focus on the lessons learned from failure, and use them to improve your performance and develop your skills.

> **Perception of effort:** People with a growth mindset value effort as an integral part of learning. It's understood that hard work and dedication are essential for developing their abilities. Conversely, those with a fixed mindset see signs of weakness or inadequacy and may be more inclined to abandon their efforts.

> **Response to setbacks and failure:** Individuals with a growth mindset display resilience in the face of setbacks and failures, using them as opportunities for learning and personal growth. Those with a fixed mindset are more likely to give up or become disheartened when encountering setbacks or failures.

> **View of effort:** Individuals with a growth mindset regard effort and hard work as essential to achieving success and realizing their full potential. In contrast, those with a fixed mindset may perceive effort as unnecessary or futile if they believe their abilities are fixed.

> **Acceptance of criticism:** Individuals with a growth mindset are receptive to constructive criticism. In contrast, those with a fixed mindset may resist criticism or feedback, fearing that it will expose their limitations and inadequacies.

*

Developing a growth mindset can be challenging, but with the right strategies and mindset, it is possible to cultivate a growth mindset that can transform your life. In this section, I will explore practical strategies for developing a growth mindset, including cultivating self-awareness, setting goals, seeking feedback, the role of positive self-talk, and identifying negative self-talk patterns.

CULTIVATING SELF-AWARENESS

Self-awareness is an essential first step in developing a growth mindset. It involves understanding your own strengths and weaknesses, recognizing your biases and assumptions, and being honest with yourself about your limitations. Self-awareness allows you to identify areas for growth and improvement and take action to develop your skills and abilities.

One way to cultivate self-awareness is to engage in reflective practices, such as journaling, meditation, or self-reflection. These practices can help you to gain insight into your thoughts, feelings, and behaviors and identify areas for growth and improvement.

SETTING GOALS

Setting goals is a key component of developing a growth mindset. Goals provide direction and focus and can help you to stay motivated and committed to your personal and professional development. When setting goals, it is important to choose goals that are specific, measurable, achievable, relevant, and time-bound (SMART).

Set goals that focus on personal and professional development. Identify areas for growth and improvement, and set goals that will help you to develop new skills and abilities. When seeking feedback, be open and receptive to constructive criticism. Ask for feedback from trusted colleagues, mentors, or friends, and use their feedback to improve your performance and develop your skills. Avoid becoming defensive or dismissive of feedback, and instead, use it as an opportunity to learn and grow.

THE ROLE OF POSITIVE SELF-TALK IN MINDSET

Positive self-talk is the practice of intentionally using positive statements and affirmations to influence your thoughts and beliefs about yourself. It involves replacing negative self-talk with positive, encouraging, and empowering language that supports personal growth and development.

By engaging in positive self-talk, you are rewiring your brain to embrace a more positive outlook on yourself and your abilities, which can profoundly influence your overall mindset and perspective on life—you are essentially reinforcing positive beliefs about yourself, which can help you feel more confident and capable.

IDENTIFY NEGATIVE SELF-TALK PATTERNS

Start by paying attention to your inner dialogue and identifying any negative or self-defeating thoughts. Write down these negative thoughts and try to reframe them in a positive and empowering way.

For example, if you catch yourself thinking, "I'm not good enough," try reframing it to, "I am capable and deserving of success."

To cultivate positive self-talk, start by paying attention to your inner dialogue and identifying any negative or self-defeating thoughts. Replace those thoughts with positive affirmations and statements that support your personal growth and development. Practice repeating these affirmations regularly, whether through journaling, meditation, or simply repeating them to yourself throughout the day.

More examples of positive affirmations include "I am powerful and capable," "I trust my intuition and make decisions with confidence," and "I am worthy of love and respect."

Mindfulness helps you cultivate awareness of your thoughts and emotions and promote self-acceptance and self-compassion. Practice mindfulness through meditation, yoga, or simply taking time to focus on your breath and observe your thoughts without judgment.

Embrace the limitless possibilities that a growth mindset offers. Remember that challenges are your opportunities, setbacks are your stepping stones, and self-belief is your greatest ally. As you cultivate positive self-talk and mindfulness, watch your inner world transform and witness its ripple effect on your outer reality.

CHAPTER 8

SETTING REALISTIC GOALS

WOMEN FACE CHALLENGES in various aspects of life, such as the workplace, personal relationships, caregiving, and societal expectations. A balanced life is possible by setting realistic goals, preventing burnout, and avoiding being overwhelmed. This process of establishing attainable objectives fosters confidence and self-esteem. Now, let's explore concrete examples of such goals on our journey.

IMPROVE A SPECIFIC SKILL

Women can set a goal to improve a specific skill that is relevant to their personal or professional development. For example, they can aim to improve their public speaking skills, learn a new programming language, or become more proficient in a particular software application.

TIME MANAGEMENT

An achievable objective involves enhancing time management skills to balance and prioritize responsibilities effectively. This is accomplished through the establishment of specific, attainable deadlines, the utilization of organizational tools like calendars and to-do lists, and the practice of delegating tasks when feasible. By honing these skills, individuals can streamline their daily routines, boost productivity, and ultimately create more time for personal growth and fulfillment, resulting in a more harmonious and fulfilling life.

FINANCIAL

By taking these proactive steps, women can secure their financial future and pave the way for greater economic freedom and peace of mind. Paying off debts ensures reduced financial burdens while creating and sticking to budgets promotes responsible spending and savings habits. Consistently saving a fixed amount each month builds a financial safety net and allows for future investments, empowering women to make informed financial decisions and navigate life's uncertainties confidently.

LEADERSHIP SKILLS

Women can embark on a journey to enhance their leadership abilities by embracing new responsibilities, actively pursuing leadership training programs, and refining their skills in communication and decision-making. Engaging in these activities equips them with the tools and knowledge needed to excel in leadership roles, whether in their careers, community involvement, or personal relationships. By consistently honing these abilities, women can achieve their leadership aspirations and inspire and empower others, fostering positive change and progress in various spheres of life.

SETTING REALISTIC GOALS TO BREAK FORTH

Goal setting provides women a clear roadmap for personal and professional growth, enabling them to concentrate on meaningful objectives. Here, we will delve into four crucial strategies for establishing realistic goals that empower women to break through barriers and succeed.

IDENTIFY YOUR VALUES AND PRIORITIES

The first step in setting realistic goals is to identify your values and priorities. What is most important to you in life? What are your long-term aspirations? What are your short-term needs and wants? By recognizing what matters to you, your goals will align with your values and priorities, giving you a clear sense of a LoP.

DEFINE SMART GOALS

SMART goals are specific, measurable, achievable, relevant, and time-bound. When setting goals, make sure they meet these criteria. Specific goals are clear and well-defined, while measurable goals have a quantifiable target. Achievable goals are realistic and attainable, while relevant goals align with your values and priorities. Finally, time-bound goals have a specific deadline, creating a sense of urgency and motivation to achieve them.

SMALLER TASKS

Breaking down your goals into smaller tasks makes them more manageable and achievable. Divide your goals into smaller steps or milestones, and set deadlines for each one—this allows you to track your progress and adjust your approach if necessary. Additionally, completing each small task gives you a sense of accomplishment and momentum, which can help keep you motivated.

FOCUS ON WHAT YOU CAN CONTROL

There may be external factors that impact your progress, but you can control your own actions and behaviors. Focus on what you can do to rather than worrying about factors outside of your control. This approach will help you stay motivated and empowered, even in challenging circumstances.

Remember that positive self-talk and affirmations are like the wind beneath your wings, keeping you soaring high even in turbulent skies. As we explore the importance of celebrating milestones throughout this journey, don't merely tell yourself to acknowledge your progress – show yourself the appreciation you deserve.

Share your achievements with friends and family, indulge in a well-deserved treat, or take a serene moment to reflect on the remarkable journey you've embarked upon. After all, the seeds of your future successes are sown in these moments of celebration.

CHAPTER 9

MAKING A DIFFERENCE

WOMEN HAVE HISTORICALLY been underrepresented and undervalued in many areas of society, but today, women are breaking through barriers and making a difference. From activism and advocacy to leadership and innovation, women are making a positive impact in a variety of fields.

Here are some ways that women can make a difference in the world, some that we have already touched on. At the end of the chapter, ten interactive questions will help you note where you are making a difference.

ADVOCATE FOR CAUSES

Women can use their voices and their influence to advocate for causes they care about, such as gender equality, environmental protection, or social justice. By raising awareness and mobilizing others, women can help drive positive change in their communities and beyond.

LEAD WITH COMPASSION

Women have a unique perspective on leadership, often prioritizing empathy, collaboration, and relationship-building. By leading with compassion, women can create inclusive and supportive environments that empower others to achieve their full potential.

INNOVATE AND DISRUPT

Women are breaking through barriers in fields such as technology, science, and entrepreneurship, bringing new perspectives and approaches to traditionally male-dominated fields. By innovating and disrupting the status quo, women can challenge assumptions and create new possibilities for themselves and others.

VOLUNTEER AND DONATE

Women can make a meaningful impact by dedicating their time and resources to organizations that align with their values and priorities. By actively supporting causes close to their hearts, women can enhance the effectiveness of these organizations and play a vital role in driving positive change.

PURSUE A CAREER IN PUBLIC SERVICE

Women can make a difference by pursuing careers in public services, such as politics, law, or social work. By working in these fields, women can help shape policy and create systems that promote fairness, justice, and equality.

FINDING FULFILLMENT AND HAPPINESS

As a woman, finding fulfillment and happiness can be a complex journey that is influenced by many factors, including personal values, relationships, career aspirations, and self-care. Here are some strategies that can help women find fulfillment and happiness in their lives.

> **Identify personal values:** Understanding personal values can provide a foundation for a fulfilling life. By reflecting on what is most important to them, women can make decisions and take actions that align with their values and give them a sense of purpose.

> **Foster positive relationships:** Positive relationships with family, friends, and romantic partners can contribute to happiness and fulfillment. By nurturing supportive relationships, women can feel connected, valued, and loved.

> **Pursue meaningful work:** Work that aligns with personal values and provides a sense of purpose can contribute to fulfillment and happiness. By pursuing careers or volunteer opportunities that are meaningful to them, women can feel a sense of accomplishment and satisfaction.

> **Engage in hobbies and interests:** Pursuing hobbies and interests that bring joy and fulfillment can help women find balance and meaning in their lives. By engaging in activities that they enjoy, women can reduce stress and increase positive emotions.

Finding fulfillment and happiness as a woman involves a combination of self-reflection, self-care, positive relationships, meaningful work, and engaging in activities that bring joy and fulfillment. By identifying personal values, fostering positive relationships, pursuing meaningful work, practicing self-care, engaging in hobbies and interests, embracing a growth mindset, and practicing gratitude, women can cultivate a fulfilling and happy life.

Review

1. What has been the historical representation of women in various societal areas, and how has this representation evolved? What has been your experience?

2. In what ways are women breaking through barriers to make a positive impact in today's world? How do you break through?

3. How can women advocate for causes they care about, and why is advocacy important? What do you advocate?

4. What unique qualities do women often bring to leadership roles, and how can leading with compassion benefit organizations and communities? What are your examples?

5. How do women contribute to innovation in traditionally male-dominated fields, and how does this impact those industries?

6. Why is volunteering and donating resources to causes aligned with one's values considered a meaningful way for women to make a difference? How do you volunteer?

7. How can women pursuing careers in public service, such as politics or social work, influence policy and promote fairness, justice, and equality? Write down as many examples as you can from your experiences.

8. What factors can influence a woman's journey toward finding fulfillment and happiness in her life?

9. Why is identifying personal values important in achieving a fulfilling life, and how can one align one's actions with these values?

10. How can positive relationships with family, friends, and romantic partners contribute to a woman's overall happiness and fulfillment, and how can these relationships be nurtured? What are your examples?

CHAPTER 10

TIPS AND EXERCISES

LET ME GUIDE YOU through the tips you need to gain more clarity and direction on your journey to finding purpose as a woman.

TIP 1. REFLECT ON YOUR PASSIONS AND INTERESTS
Take some time to think about the activities and hobbies that bring you joy and fulfillment.

> What subjects or topics do you find yourself gravitating towards? What are your favorite books or movies?

> By exploring your interests and passions, you can begin to identify potential career paths or areas of focus that align with your values and strengths. What did you learn about your passions and interests?

TIP 2. IDENTIFY YOUR VALUES
Another essential step in finding purpose is identifying your values. What do you care about most in life? What are your priorities? By identifying your values, you can begin to make decisions that align with your beliefs and goals. You may also find it helpful to create a

personal mission statement or vision board that reflects your values and aspirations.

> What did you learn about your identity and values?

TIP 3. EXPLORE DIFFERENT CAREER PATHS

Exploring different career paths can help you gain clarity and direction on your journey to finding purpose. Take some time to research various industries and fields. Consider shadowing or interning in areas that interest you. You may also find it helpful to take career assessments or personality tests to gain insight into your strengths and potential career paths.

> What did you learn?

TIP 4. EMBRACE YOUR UNIQUE PATH

Remember that finding purpose is a unique journey, and there is no one right way to do it. Embrace your unique path and trust the process. You may need to try different things and make mistakes along the way, but these experiences will ultimately help you gain clarity and direction.

> What did you learn when you embraced your unique path in the past?

TIP 5. TAKE ACTION

Finally, taking action is essential for gaining clarity and direction on your journey to finding purpose. Make a plan and take steps towards your goals, even if they are small ones. Celebrate your progress along the way, and don't be afraid to adjust your plans as needed.

> What happened when you took action?

EXERCISES

At the end of each question, write down everything you've learned.
Try something new every week

One of the best ways to break out of your comfort zone is to try something new every week. This could be as simple as trying a new food or listening to a new genre of music, or it could be something more significant like taking a dance class or learning a new language. By trying new things, you can expand your horizons and gain new perspectives on life.

> **Set goals and take action:** Setting goals and taking action toward them is another great way to break out of your comfort zone. Identify one or two goals that are outside of your comfort zone and take steps towards achieving them. Sign up for a new class or starting your own business. By taking action toward your goals, you can build confidence and develop new skills and experiences.

> **Take some risks:** Taking risks is another essential exercise for breaking out of your comfort zone: Speaking up in a meeting, asking for a promotion, or starting a new business venture. While taking risks can be scary, it can also lead to significant rewards and opportunities for growth.

> **Face your fears:** Facing your fears is another essential exercise for breaking out of your comfort zone. Identify the things that scare you the most, and then take steps to face them. This could mean taking a public speaking course or skydiving. By facing your fears, you can gain confidence and overcome limiting beliefs that may be holding you back.

> **Challenge your negative self-talk:** Negative self-talk can be a significant barrier to breaking out of your comfort zone. When we tell ourselves that we're not good enough or that we can't do something, we limit ourselves and prevent ourselves from taking on new challenges. Challenge your negative self-talk by replacing

negative thoughts with positive affirmations. For example, if you catch yourself thinking, "I'm not good enough to do that," replace it with, "I am capable and confident."

> **Practice mindfulness:** Practicing mindfulness is another exercise that can help you break out of your comfort zone. Mindfulness involves being present at the moment and fully experiencing your thoughts and feelings without judgment. By practicing mindfulness, you can become more aware of your comfort zone and learn to step outside of it when necessary.

> **Volunteer or give back:** Volunteering or giving back is another way to break out of your comfort zone and find purpose in life. Volunteer at a local shelter, donating to a charity, or mentoring someone in need. By giving back, you can gain a sense of fulfillment and purpose while making a positive impact on the world.

> **Practice gratitude:** By redirecting your attention towards gratitude, you can avoid the constraints and apprehensions that often hold you back. Instead, you can channel your energy towards the vast possibilities and opportunities that await. This transformative shift in focus can catalyze personal growth and positive change. One practical way to incorporate gratitude into your daily life is to set aside a few moments each day for reflection. Take this time to ponder and appreciate the things you're grateful for. Keep a gratitude journal where you jot down these reflections or share them with a trusted friend or family member.

> **Surround yourself with positive people**: Surrounding yourself with positive people has been discussed in previous chapters. Spend time with people who support and encourage you to step outside of your comfort zone and pursue your goals. By surrounding yourself with positive people, you can gain a sense

of community and support while also gaining the courage to take risks and pursue your dreams.

BREAK FORTH

I HOPE YOU ARE filled with inspiration and a newfound sense of empowerment, ready to embark on a journey of self-discovery as a woman. Throughout these pages, we've delved into the myriad challenges that many women encounter when seeking a LoP. We've also explored effective strategies and shifts in mindset that can assist you in surmounting these obstacles and unlocking your full potential.

At the core of this book lies a fundamental belief: that every woman possesses the boundless potential and the ability to turn her dreams into reality while leading a life that resonates with her purpose and values.

Embracing a growth mindset entails a greater readiness to take risks, learn from failures, and pursue your dreams with unwavering passion and persistence. Cultivating a growth mindset can be a formidable endeavor.

It necessitates a willingness to challenge your existing beliefs and biases, embrace discomfort and uncertainty, and push through the fear and self-doubt that may be holding you back. It also entails an unwavering commitment to continuous learning and personal growth and a readiness to seek mentors and role models who can support and guide your journey.

I implore you to approach your goals and dreams with intention, zeal, and unwavering determination. Always remember that your potential as a woman knows no bounds, and you possess the capability to accomplish anything.

If you ever feel stuck or overwhelmed, return to this guide and revisit the strategies and mindset shifts we've explored together. Reconnect with your sense of purpose and deeply-held values, and remind yourself of the limitless potential that resides within you as a woman.

Everything you require for greatness is already within you—all that remains is for you to believe in yourself, take bold action, and steadfastly pursue your dreams. March forth with courage, confidence, and resolve, knowing that you can attain anything you set your sights on—your purpose and greatness are there, waiting to be claimed.

ABOUT THE AUTHOR

Lutaline Fosah

Lutaline Fosah is an entrepreneur and very passionate about the affairs of women and young girls. She founded Tribestrong, a brand that empowers women to go after their purpose and embrace themselves. She also founded the GirlStrong Mentoring Program, a Non-Profit Organization mentoring young girls ages 7-15 to empower them to be confident and brave and equip them with the tools needed to navigate life.

Lutaline is a Law school graduate, a nurse, a wife, and a mother of three children. She attended most of her education in West Africa in Cameroon and later moved to America, where she resides with her family.